Tiger Woods

VS.

Jack Nicklaus

BY TOM GLAVE

SportsZone

An Imprint of Abdo Publishing
abdopublishing.com

abdopublishing.com

Published by Abdo Publishing, a division of ABDO, PO Box 398166, Minneapolis, Minnesota 55439. Copyright © 2018 by Abdo Consulting Group, Inc. International copyrights reserved in all countries. No part of this book may be reproduced in any form without written permission from the publisher. SportsZone™ is a trademark and logo of Abdo Publishing.

Printed in the United States of America, North Mankato, Minnesota
102017
012018

Cover Photos: Mark J. Terrill/AP Images, left; Phil Sandlin/AP Images, right
Interior Photos: AP Images, 4–5, 8, 11, 27; Mark Lennihan/AP Images, 5; Lenny Ignelzi/ AP Images, 6–7; Rick Scuteri/AP Images, 8–9; Robert Huntzinger/Sports Illustrated/ Getty Images, 12–13; Scott Halleran/Getty Images Sport/Getty Images, 15; Rob Carr/AP Images, 16; Doug Mills/AP Images, 17; Elise Amendola/AP Images, 18–19; Phil Sandlin/AP Images, 21; Charlie Riedel/AP Images, 23; Bettmann/Getty Images, 24–25; Morry Gash/AP Images, 29

Editor: Patrick Donnelly
Series Designer: Sarah Winkler

Publisher's Cataloging-in-Publication Data
Names: Glave, Tom, author.
Title: Tiger Woods vs. Jack Nicklaus / by Tom Glave.
Other titles: Tiger Woods versus Jack Nicklaus
Description: Minneapolis, Minnesota : Abdo Publishing, 2018. | Series: Versus | Includes online resources and index.
Identifiers: LCCN 2017946933 | ISBN 9781532113598 (lib.bdg.) | ISBN 9781532152474 (ebook)
Subjects: LCSH: Golfers--Juvenile literature. | Golf--Records--Juvenile literature. | Sports--History--Juvenile literature.
Classification: DDC 796.352--dc23
LC record available at https://lccn.loc.gov/2017946933

TABLE OF CONTENTS

INTRODUCTION

Golf is a unique sport in that its players aren't competing against each other. In golf your competition is the course, the weather conditions, your emotions and attitude, and sometimes history itself.

Jack Nicklaus and Tiger Woods are undoubtedly two of the best golfers ever. They played in different eras, used different equipment, competed on different courses, and faced different levels of scrutiny. Yet both achieved levels of greatness most can only dream of attaining.

Which one was better? It's an argument without a right or wrong answer. We'll tell their stories and lay out the facts.

JACK OR TIGER?
YOU DECIDE!

Tiger Woods launches a tee shot during the second round of the 1997 Masters.

CHAPTER 1

OFF THE TEE

Golf fans were eager to see how Tiger Woods would fare in his first major tournament. They had been hearing stories about the 21-year-old prodigy for years. Woods had turned pro in August 1996 and won three Professional Golfers' Association (PGA) Tour events in his first eight months.

In April 1997, he stood on the tee box at the Masters Tournament. The Masters is one of professional golf's four major championships. It is played at Augusta National Golf Club in Georgia every year, and the winner receives an iconic green jacket as a prize.

Woods's booming tee shots electrified the crowd at the Masters. He averaged 323 yards off the tee during the tournament, 25 yards longer than any other player.

Jack Nicklaus tees off at the second hole of Augusta National during the 1978 Masters.

He even impressed legendary golfer Jack Nicklaus.

"He's so long, he reduces the course to nothing," Nicklaus said. "Absolutely nothing."

Nicklaus knew about big drives. He was one of the longest and straightest off the tee during the 1960s and 1970s.

The PGA Tour did not keep as many statistics during Nicklaus's prime as it does today. Nicklaus led the tour with an average driving distance of 276 yards during 11 tracked events in 1968, near the prime of his career. He averaged 269 yards in 1980, when the PGA Tour started keeping records. Woods's best average was 316.1 yards in 2005. Keep in mind, golf balls and clubs have changed over the years. This allows golfers today to hit longer and straighter because of the weight and design of the equipment.

Nicklaus was a great athlete. He played multiple sports growing up. That helped him develop his strength and coordination, which gave him an advantage over other golfers. He used his strong legs and sturdy body to hit long, high fades.

Nicklaus worried more about his accuracy than distance. He wanted to set up his next shot in the best possible position. Sometimes he sacrificed length for a better landing. Nicklaus's famous fade drifted from left to right. It had height and a soft landing. This helped him get his tee shots to a specific place.

Woods is also very strong. He gets great power from his big arms and strong core. This produces amazing swing speed.

As he aged, Woods added muscle to his lanky frame to generate even more power with his drives.

MEET THE PLAYERS

JACK NICKLAUS

- Born January 21, 1940, in Columbus, Ohio
- 5 feet, 11 inches/190 pounds
- Attended Ohio State University, 1960–61
- Home today: North Palm Beach, Florida

TIGER WOODS

- Born December 30, 1975, in Cypress, California
- 6 feet, 1 inch/185 pounds
- Attended Stanford University, 1994–96
- Home today: Hobe Sound, Florida

Woods is known for his intense workout routine. His athletic ability made other professional golfers realize they had to focus on improving their strength.

Each player blasted numerous long drives their fans and opponents will likely never forget. The PGA Championship featured a long-drive contest before the 1963 tournament started. Nicklaus won the event with a 341-yard drive. He won a money clip that he still uses. He also won the PGA Championship that year.

Woods holds a world record for the longest drive on the PGA Tour. He hit a tee shot 498 yards at the 2002 Mercedes Championship on No. 18 at the Plantation Course at Kapalua Resort in Hawaii. The 663-yard hole is the PGA Tour's longest and plays downhill and with the wind, setting up lots of monster drives.

Their long drives weren't just for show, however. They were crucial parts of each player's success. One of Nicklaus's most famous tee shots helped him win his record 18th major when he was 46 years old. Nicklaus hit a 5-iron right at the flag of No. 16 at the 1986 Masters. He knew the shot was on target. He bent to pick up his tee rather than watch it land. The ball landed on the green just three feet from the pin. Nicklaus made the birdie putt and went on to win by one stroke over Tom Kite and Greg Norman.

Woods's memorable drives showed off his power and distance. His monster drive on No. 18 at the 2001 Masters is a good example. He held his finish longer so he could watch the beautiful shot sail out of sight. The win gave Woods consecutive wins in the four major tournaments—a feat that came to be known as the "Tiger Slam."

Nicklaus holds the champion's trophy after he won the 1972 US Open at Pebble Beach.

Nicklaus shows off his touch with a fairway iron at the 1962 US Open, which he went on to win in a playoff for his first major title.

CHAPTER 2

THE APPROACH

Professional golfers have a choice to make before every shot. They can carry 14 golf clubs during a round, and each can deliver a different result. A typical bag includes a driver, a 3-wood, a 5-wood, eight irons, a putter, and two more clubs of their choice.

Nicklaus had a big decision to make as a tour rookie in 1962. He was facing golf legend Arnold Palmer in an 18-hole playoff at the US Open at Oakmont Country Club outside of Pittsburgh. Nicklaus led by two strokes heading to the 18th hole, but a bad drive left him in the fairway rough. However, Palmer's second shot found the rough short of the green. That allowed Nicklaus to play cautiously.

PROFESSIONAL SUCCESS

JACK NICKLAUS

- Professional debut: 1962 Los Angeles Open
- Years active: 1962–2005
- PGA Tour victories: 73
- Major victories: 18 (6 Masters, 5 PGA Championships, 4 US Opens, 3 British Opens)

TIGER WOODS

- Professional debut: 1996 Greater Milwaukee Open
- Years active: 1996–present
- PGA Tour victories: 79
- Major victories: 14 (4 Masters, 4 PGA Championships, 3 US Opens, 3 British Opens)

He used a pitching wedge to get back onto the fairway before hitting a solid 9-iron. The ball landed 12 feet from the hole, leaving Nicklaus an easy two-putt to win his first tournament as a professional.

Long irons don't loft the ball in the air as much, but they can provide distance. The shorter irons, numbered 8 and 9, don't send the ball as far. But they can lift the ball high into the air. That will cut down on how far it rolls after landing. Shorter irons won't hook or slice as much, because loft eliminates some spin.

Nicklaus and Woods used their irons from all over the hole to get the ball to the green. These approach shots are some of the most important because they can set up short putts.

A plaque marks the spot where Nicklaus stood when he hit his famous 1-iron on the final hole of the 1967 US Open at Baltusrol.

Nicklaus and Woods were both confident with their long irons. Nicklaus has said there's very little difference between them in their iron play.

Nicklaus's fade shot kept him straight, and he didn't like to take chances as he approached the green. His choice of shot from the fairway was one that set up a makeable putt.

One example came at the 1967 US Open at Baltusrol Golf Club in New Jersey. Nicklaus pulled his tee shot into the thick rough on the par-5 No. 18. He had to pitch back to the fairway 238 yards from the hole. He needed a perfect approach shot to give him a chance at a birdie. His high-flying, uphill 1-iron landed on the green just 22 feet from the hole. Nicklaus sunk the putt for a birdie, giving him a win and tournament record score of 275.

Woods did some of his best work with long irons in fairway bunkers.

Woods's great skill off the tee allowed him to be more aggressive. Sometimes it set up short approach shots. But sometimes, when it went wrong, he needed a recovery.

Many consider Woods's approach on the final hole at Glen Abbey Golf Club one of his best shots ever. Holding a one-shot lead over Grant Waite at the 2000 Bell Canadian Open, Woods's tee shot on the par-5 No. 18 found a fairway bunker. He was 213 yards from the pin, with lake between him and the green. The safe play would be to lay up—hit it short of the green. Instead Woods smoked a 6-iron to the back of the green. Woods then chipped close and sank the birdie putt to win by a stroke.

Woods and Nicklaus have both said their best shots in competition were irons. Woods's came on the par-4 18th hole at Hazeltine National in Minnesota during the 2002 PGA Championship. His tee shot during the second round hooked and found the edge of a fairway bunker 200 yards from the hole. He had an awkward stance above the ball, and a tree was directly in front of him. Woods blasted a 3-iron out of the sand. The ball hooked around the tree and landed the ball eight feet from the hole for a birdie putt.

Nicklaus came up big on No. 15 at Augusta during the 1975 Masters. A huge tee shot on the par-5 hole left Nicklaus in the fairway 246 yards from the flag. He nailed his 1-iron and thought it might fly into the hole. It rolled past the cup, and Nicklaus missed the eagle putt, but he made birdie and went on to win by one stroke.

Woods hits what he calls one of his best shots ever, a 3-iron out of a fairway bunker during the 2002 PGA Championship at Hazeltine.

Woods's brilliance around the green gave him many moments to celebrate, such as this reaction after winning the 2005 Masters.

CHAPTER 3

THE SHORT GAME

The goal in golf is to get the ball into the hole in the fewest strokes. After the big shots from the tee and fairway, a golfer must finish around the hole. A solid short game can help create low scores—and some of the sport's most memorable moments.

Woods demonstrated that regularly on some of the game's biggest stages. On the final day of the 2005 Masters, he had a one-shot lead over Chris DiMarco heading to the par-3 No. 16. Woods's tee shot went long into the rough. Instead of chipping to the short part of the green, Woods skipped a shot 25 feet above the hole, hoping the slope would bring the ball back. His strategy worked. The ball slowly rolled back to the hole, stopped momentarily at the lip of the cup, and then fell in for an incredible birdie. That shot helped Woods win his fourth Masters.

Golfers use special clubs to pitch or chip from short distances. A pitch is a short shot that flies high in the air and lands on the green with little roll. A chip pops the ball into the air and rolls a longer distance on the green.

Nicklaus admits Woods had the better short game. Nicklaus said he was so confident in his long irons and putting that he did not focus much on his short irons early in his career.

Putting requires a whole different set of skills. Once on the green, a golfer needs confidence and the ability to read the green. The physical characteristics of the green—slopes, grass type, moisture—can influence a putt.

Nicklaus always seemed poised over putts. His approach on the green was similar to his tee and fairway shots. He aimed to pick out the proper speed to leave the shortest possible second putt. He avoided stressful and difficult short putts by being conservative.

"I was a fine two-putter, but sometimes too defensive—too concerned about three-putting—to go for putts that I probably should have gone for," Nicklaus said.

Nicklaus made a slew of big shots as he rallied to win the 1986 Masters, including a 12-foot eagle putt on No. 15 and a 3-foot birdie on No. 16. Most remember a solid 18-foot putt on No. 17 that gave Nicklaus the lead. It was a tricky read, and Nicklaus discussed it for a long time with his son, Jackie, who was his caddie. Jackie suggested aiming for the left edge, but Nicklaus thought the greens were breaking more to the right than they appeared.

Nicklaus watches his famous putt roll toward the cup on the 17th hole during the final round of the 1986 Masters.

He was right. He aimed just right of the hole, and the ball went straight into the cup. Nicklaus knew it, lifting his putter in celebration before the ball trickled in. CBS announcer Verne Lundquist famously shouted "Yes, sir!" at the perfect shot.

JACK NICKLAUS

- First major won: 1962 US Open
- Career highlight: Nicklaus sank an 8-foot birdie putt to win the 1959 US Amateur Championship.
- Awards:
  --PGA Tour Rookie of the Year (1962)
  --PGA Player of the Year (1967, 1972, 1973, 1975, 1976)
  --PGA Golf Professional Hall of Fame
  --ESPY Lifetime Achievement Award (2001)

TIGER WOODS

- First major won: 1997 Masters
- Career highlight: In 2000 and 2001, Woods became the first player to win the four majors consecutively.
- Awards:
  --PGA Tour Rookie of the Year (1996)
  --PGA Player of the Year (1997, 1999–2003, 2005–07, 2009, 2013)
  --ESPY Best Male Athlete (1997, 1999–2001)

Nicklaus was a legend on the greens in Augusta. He drained a 40-foot putt for a birdie on No. 16 on the way to winning the 1975 Masters. He said he knew it was in with 12 feet left and leapt for joy when it fell in.

But Woods has a long list of amazing finishes as well. He made a 40-foot birdie putt to beat Ernie Els in a playoff at the 2000 Mercedes Championship. A 60-foot downhill putt for a birdie during the third round of the 2001 Players Championship put him on track for that title.

Woods chipped in from an awkward lie in the greenside rough during the third round of the 2008 US Open at Torrey Pines. His shot bounced on the 17th green and dunked into the hole for birdie. The next day, Woods drained a 15-foot birdie putt on No. 18 to force a playoff with Rocco Mediate. He celebrated with a double fist pump. Woods won the tournament the next day despite playing all weekend on an injured left knee that required surgery.

Woods watches a putt during the fourth round of the 2008 US Open.

Palmer, *left*, smiles as the 22-year-old Nicklaus is interviewed at the 1962 US Open. Nicklaus defeated Palmer in an 18-hole playoff to win his first major.

CHAPTER 4

IN THE CLUTCH

Jack Nicklaus was a rookie professional golfer in 1962. Arnold Palmer was the king of golf at the time. Palmer had five major championships under his belt, including the 1962 Masters.

Nicklaus and Palmer were paired together during the first two rounds of the 1962 US Open. The Open was being played at Oakmont, just 40 miles (64 km) from Palmer's hometown of Latrobe, Pennsylvania.

The crowd wanted to see Palmer win another major tournament. They did not want to see the young up-and-comer beat their hero.

"Arnie's Army" was tough on Nicklaus. They heckled and called him names. They cheered if he hit a poor shot. They stomped their feet to make the ground shake.

Nicklaus ignored it all. He concentrated on his game, handled the pressure well, and beat Palmer in a playoff to win his first major championship.

"To me, pressure . . . was what you live for or why you play the game," Nicklaus said. "As much as I love the game of golf, I loved the competition as much or more."

Nicklaus and Woods proved throughout their careers they could handle pressure. They made big shots when they needed them. They found ways to win.

Nicklaus and Woods have more major championship wins than any other golfers. Both men knew how to close out those weekends with a trophy in hand.

Woods won 14 majors through 2016. He had the lead going into the final round of a major tournament 15 times. He lost the lead only once. Nicklaus won a record 18 major tournaments during his career. He led or shared the lead after three rounds during 12 majors. He won 10 of them.

Nicklaus rallied on the final day of a major eight times, including his first at the 1962 US Open and his last at the 1986 Masters. His first British Open victory, at Muirfield in Scotland in 1966, was another great comeback. Nicklaus entered the final round in second place. He took control early and sealed the win with spectacular iron play.

Nicklaus needed to finish with a birdie and par to beat Dave Thomas and Doug Sanders. He used a 5-iron for his second shot on the par-5 No. 17, landing the ball 20 feet short of the green. It rolled out of sight, but the crowd's reaction told Nicklaus it was a great shot. It stopped 15 feet from the cup, and Nicklaus two-putted for birdie.

A 3-iron on the par-4 No. 18 set up another two-putt for the one-stroke win. It gave Nicklaus the career Grand Slam, meaning he had won all four majors at least once.

Woods's intense focus on the course and his big wins helped him intimidate other players. They weren't sure they could compete with a golfer who made so many amazing shots. Woods claimed he didn't feel the pressure, especially in the clutch. He developed a superstition of sorts, always wearing a red shirt for the final round of a tournament. When opponents saw him stalking the course in his "Sunday red" they usually knew they were in for a long day.

Nicklaus digs himself out of a tough spot of rough at the 1966 British Open at Muirfield. He went on to win, giving him the career Grand Slam at age 26.

JACK NICKLAUS

- Important records: Most majors won (18); most wins at the Masters (6); oldest player to win the Masters (46 in 1986)
- Key rivals: Gary Player, Arnold Palmer, Tom Watson, Lee Trevino, Seve Ballesteros
- Off-course accomplishments: Designed 298 courses through Nicklaus Design; founded the Memorial Tournament, which donates to charities; wrote several books

"I knew exactly how intimidating I was, and I've got to tell you, it was a tremendous advantage."

— Jack Nicklaus

TIGER WOODS

- Important records: Widest margin of victory at a major (15 strokes, 2000 US Open); most consecutive weeks as top-ranked golfer (264); most consecutive events without missing the cut (142)
- Key rivals: Phil Mickelson, Ernie Els, David Duval, Sergio García, Vijay Singh, Rory McIlroy
- Off-course accomplishments: Provides community-based programs for children through the Tiger Woods Foundation; designed 10 courses through TGR Design; wrote a best-selling golf instruction book

"I get to play golf for a living. What more can you ask for— getting paid for doing what you love."

— Tiger Woods

Wearing his red shirt, Woods made a 25-foot birdie putt on the final hole to win the 2008 Arnold Palmer Invitational at Bay Hill. He did the same thing a year later, draining a 12-foot birdie. And his 15-foot birdie putt on the final hole of the 2008 US Open to force a playoff is one of his greatest clutch shots.

"Your senses are heightened when you're in a clutch situation," Woods said. "You just feel if you believe in something so hard, if you truly believe . . . the ball will go in."

Phil Mickelson, *left*, helps Woods into the classic green jacket in 2005 after Woods's fourth Masters championship.

GLOSSARY

BIRDIE
A score in which a golfer finishes a hole one shot under par.

BUNKER
A hazard on the golf course, usually a hole filled with sand.

EAGLE
A score on a hole that is two strokes under par.

FADE
A shot that curves from left to right for a right-handed golfer.

FAIRWAY
A long stretch of mowed grass that connects the tee to the green.

HECKLE
To harass or bother a performer by saying rude things.

HOOK
A shot that curves from right to left for a right-handed golfer.

PAR
The number of shots a golfer is expected to need to finish a hole.

PRODIGY
A young person with exceptional talent.

ROOKIE
A professional athlete in his or her first year of competition.

ROUGH
Longer grass that grows at the edge of a fairway.

STATISTICS
Data collected in the form of numbers.

ONLINE RESOURCES

Booklinks
NONFICTION NETWORK
FREE! ONLINE NONFICTION RESOURCES

To learn more about great golfers, visit abdobooklinks.com. These links are routinely monitored and updated to provide the most current information available.

MORE INFORMATION

BOOKS

Daniel, P. K. *The Best Golfers of All Time*. Minneapolis, MN: Abdo Publishing, 2015.

Howell, Brian. *The Masters*. Minneapolis, MN: Abdo Publishing, 2013.

Williams, Doug. *Tiger Woods Makes Masters History*. Minneapolis, MN: Abdo Publishing, 2015.

Index

About the Author

Tom Glave learned to write about sports at the University of Missouri. He has written about sports for newspapers in New Jersey, Missouri, Arkansas, and Texas. He has also written several books about sports. He looks forward to teaching his four children about all sports.